I0161586

ANDREA HENCHEY

GIRL TALKS TO THIS THISTLE

Thistle, you apostle of a—
you epistle of a— you are
sharp-leaved, spine-tipped—
mute.
            Speak!
Pluck. Prick. Purple epistle: a letter from whom?
Even the goldfinch cannot read you.

Your ball-shaped flowerhead has a mind
or not, that thinks or not, not speaking, not
a single word.

Please, bright messenger, weed:
            words are what I need.
Thistle, apostle, epistle of the dirt.

I do not know your language.

What, thistle, if you could, would you say?
Like the lilies: *never toil nor spin*?

Maybe: Be silent. Listen.
Finally: Be still.

ANDREW SAGE

COLONIAL MEADOWS

Birds resemble
Our tent   It was hot
    You were
Up   Everyone else
Asleep in trailers   Failures

The little rooms have
Lost their tables
    Another hour before
Breakfast is
Too much of an intention

Wretch the sun will
Make you a shadow of
    Being there
I must start
From the beginning always

Like sweet
Nectarines in season
    Your noisy belt buckle
And sinking sinking sinking
Spoil me

A wren unsettled
The top of our
    Pitch pine   Many a year
Planted in that tree   Okay
Thirty

How young a tune
O sleepless bird

ASYLUM PICNIC

The tone of
Soothing is, *Shut up, it's*
Going to be okay. Reasoning is
Cold water to step into. Algae
To the ankles. A remarkable duck
Swimming away, nettles
To nettle someone.
I, too! I, too!
From 5:30am, screams of
Children. No more logic
Than meets the eye. We put apples
Into
The tree, then periodically
Rake 'em down.
Sample the olives, choose
Cheeses (feta: Greek, French, Bulgarian).
I strip to my boxers and step
Into the water
Or lie on the couch, trying to nap,
Lodged there.
The ram recognizes another ram:
Will they butt heads or engage
In a full and frank exchange of ideas?
Samuel, age 2, thinks
Everything is a strawberry:
The good news is, he will not go hungry.
I find the waiting less frustrating.
I'm very upset with you. I don't like
That you did that. Don't let it
Happen again. The fighting, the telling
In that same civilizing voice
That is the vise of command.

LISA FAY COUTLEY

ODE TO THE APPLE

Instigator of every eye, tease in red
          pleather pants, crux of the sweet
matter set to explode in the world's perfect
          faces, we understand your bad

rap. We know you're not the singer of deep
          sleeps. Who, but you, has stayed
still & taken the arrow for the head? You fall,
          you float, you pawn yourself a stunt

double, carrying only enough poison to piss
          off an ant. In fact, we praise your bad
ass. For being the cider, the sauce, the sweet
          pie with a thick crust. For keeping

teeth clean & hornets fed & doctors
          begging their bread. For holding
fast through a history of missteps, juggled
          from one sad hand to the next. You,

apple, are loneliness hung against sun, thrown
          for your dull thud & your soft insides,
a dozen plucked hearts, tossed in a bucket,
          waiting for someone to take a bite.

MY DESERT

My desert has many steeples & prays
        to no one. A fence at the flames
            of sagebrush & tumbleweed,

my desert sleeps bootheels to assbones.
        He dreams in petroglyph panels.
            When my desert travels, he steers

by the compass of a rattlesnake's tongue.
        He skins prairie dogs with a butterfly
            knife. My desert needs no canteen,

no poncho, no saddle or horse. Give him moon
        shine, filterless tobacco, the biggest belt
            buckle west of the Great Divide.

My desert believes in the power of a fault line,
        that every grain of sand will map its way
            back to the ocean. He knows

busted spines & rummaged pot shards & sun
        rusted aluminum cans. By night, he has
            summoned his widows to ruin

sites & cloaked his succulents in chickenwire.
        He's scrawled survival on the vulture's bones
            & wrung one last drop for the juniper's

root, pluming through rock. My desert pretends
        he's not a desert at all: his cracked bowl,
            his impassable walls, his lake poisoned

by salt. But my desert knows what waterless
        means. Some nights, he walks bootless
            into the cold & strikes a match

just to grow warm again. All winter long, my desert
        cups his hand to his ear, he kneels, he listens
            to those ragged peaks, where all is come

& all is lost & all is searching for the moment
     when my desert will make lakes again
               from snow, & we'll lie down & float.

SHADES

In the gray kitchen making our morning coffee
I hear the tiny chirrup of a cardinal – he's in
the false cypress' green boughs, brilliant male,
one red note in a world where color is there
if you look but the dull pall overhead makes
looking hard. Along the olive gray garage,
bronze foliage – lilies, daffodils, Siberian iris –
emerging from snow. The woman with the two
golden retrievers is down on Water Street, dogs
trailing her in the field. I haven't seen her in
months. Are there herons at the river? How we
want signs, look for auspices, haruspices, the guts
and innards of the future. In beds I can't see
beneath the porch, the viburnum's scarlet berries,
rosy flowers of hydrangea paniculata grandiflora,
the thrusting cones of oakleaf hydrangea, a shade
closer to blood. How can I leave this garden and
not grieve at its gradually being eradicated? All's
well that .... Endings are awkward, knotted, half-
heartless careless careworn worn out lingering stuck
bits and pieces of the past adhering to the here,
the new. I look out at the white scars on the sky,
the stranded repossessed car next to the disused
recycling center, the white stasis of the fields.
A small bird sounds. Having created something
that will not last, can I be reconciled to its not
lasting? Yesterday I realized I'm not walking to
the river mornings because I know I'm going
to have to leave it. How I will miss this view,
the straggling mulberry at the foot of the garden
alive with winter birds, the creek a white path
intersected by black shadow, bordering trees
paler in air than their images in water, the
vanished hills, the white expanse of sky.

SANDRA KOHLER

WINTER SUITE: DREAMS AROUND MY BROTHER

The first day of winter: temperature just
at freezing; the sky heavy, striated with
waves of gray. The light's a poor dim thing.
I am moving, with my three great-nieces,
to an apartment that's grubby, depressing.
A sink in the hallway leaks, the rooms are
small, bare, strung out along a narrow hallway,
a railway flat. The girls are complaining,
I'm calling a plumber for the leaking sink;
I find a pile of dirt someone's left on the floor,
try to sweep it up with a broom that's just
a few wisps of straw, a rusty dustpan of
twisted metal. Nothing that could work.
Did Cinderella dream of sweeping, of piles
of ash? Nothing that could work.
I am dreaming my brother's life.

     ***

The pure cold of winter, the sky unmarked
by any shadow. Venus in the southeast,
the rim of the world faintly reddening.
Family astronomy: my brother is a black hole,
my love for him a moon waxing and waning.
We are shaped by our limits, taking the form
of our fears, that prison we rail against. Looking
inward I find a mirror obscure and glittering
as the creek's surface on which ice and sky and
water are all sources of light. In it reflection
cannot be distinguished from source: what is
is solid and treacherous, deep and impenetrable,
illusion and bedrock: unexpected as weather,
obliterated and disguised by winter storms.

     ***

Driving the Garden State Parkway, my body
a corridor of pain from throat to gut: corrosive
anguish. While we're there, my brother talks
of getting better, perhaps being strong enough
to visit that old friend in the south. It's a skin on
the surface of despair. Maybe that's how we heal:

by creating that skin. I don't believe it. At home,
my dream about the serial killer who strangles
women and children goes on and on, affectless,
distanced. Unlike the intimacy, pain immediately
to hand: my brother's slow self-murder.

**

The thin top of the mulberry shivers at dawn,
hard and sharp-edged as the fallen snow turned
ice. My lame brother's obsessed with skiing again:
symbol of everything pleasurable, everything
he's lost. The ways we chafe each other are legion.
In the annals of family, the pea is always undoing
of a princess, the word profferred or withheld
a seed of alienation, disowned bonds. Needing
a scapegoat for every ill, we cast the role, forget
that the actor we assigned was yesterday the hero's
confidant, or a faithful servant, Adam to some
bluff naive Orlando; how will he play two parts?
In a dream my son tells me my brother's
his second home, love; he can't bear his
drinking himself to death. It doesn't matter
here whether my son is himself or me.

**

Waking at three something, I am full, heavy:
I am carrying my brother, a sour old man curled
into a black ball, anguished fetus in my womb.
I can't give him birth, I can't feed him, he is
shrinking, becoming harder, heavier. The deaths
I imagine delivering him will not deliver me.
The deaths I imagine delivering me will not
deliver him. In this two-faced month I look back
and remember all that I owe him, look forward
to see nothing that could rescue, ease him into
life, death. The stasis he clings to could last
forever, a gate in time, eternal paralysis.
The bird clock in the kitchen tells me
another hour has opened, a door of sand –
grains slipping through my fingers –
closed, a door of lead.

**

In the dream, my son is stricken, my husband
refuses to budge though we're late for the train,
reciting the schedule of evening departures when
we must be gone by noon. Someone dumps
crumbs into the dishwasher, over the clean dishes,
I haven't unpacked the suitcase from my last trip
and need what's in it to repack for the train I'm about
to miss. Two young girls in Amish dress water
our marriage bed, carved mahogany spread with
black velvet. We walk naked in front of our children,
siblings; we are the spirit of disorder suffusing
a house of chaos. I wake to silence and the cold
flares of sunrise, a man reading a newspaper,
peaceful, composed. The cold is an icy
medium I move through with joy.

         ***

This morning the river's white breath rises as
a trail of small clouds suspended over it, moving
south. The snow dune on the deck has shifted,
shows signs of geologic age, erosion, ancient
white stone worn by a century of wind. Great
commotion of birds, doves on the telephone wires
fat and unbalanced, swaying like dowagers.
Phoning my brother last night – afterwards
my body feels as if it has remembered old affliction,
a bout of something thought over and done with.
Waker on the threshold, Janus-like, I walk back
and forth across the barrier between yes and no,
going and coming, future and past. Double-
hearted January is the time for lightening,
discarding. For burning the letters, fasting,
refusing the offers of the past. For turning
one's back, letting the dead bury the dead.

BROMIDE

But there have been too many
answers—and none right. Thunder

seemed answer, lightning
question, but maybe both were both at once.

That so quickly
they could be, then could not, distressed him

but impressed me. We put paper bags
over our heads, walked barefoot

out into the storm. The bags yielded to rain
and plastered our faces.

We pressed holes in them to breathe.
I peeled mine off so I could see

and led him to the wheelbarrow full of water,
told him to lean over.

If pulp hadn't shielded them, his eyes
might have tried to answer rain-

and wind-troubled questions in their reflection
as I, in my way, *like lighting* I thought,

had my way.

JOHN ESTES

OBJECT PERMANENCE

Into the maple's hollow leader branch
a blur of black bird disappears;
how had I missed that large round hole,
or the industrious worry over many
days it obviously required?
I didn't think the tree that dead.
My ladder will not reach the spot
so for an hour I wait, curious what creature
I now will spare by sparing the tree,
slated as it is, was, for felling.

A boat-tailed grackle guards the margins,
swings and limns the perimeter
circuiting elm-to-shed, sycamore-to-wire-fence,
making flashy show of its crackling
caw and blue shook-foil head.

In the meantime I think about those
who walk great distances
wearing insufficient shoes;
I ache for those who ache under
the pretense that pathos is meiotic;
I say a prayer for poets
and the poems they will write,
for my next one, that there will be a next one—
but to speak of it will jinx it, so
I resign myself to sitting there,
one eye on the hole in my dying tree,
one eye marking the house's shadow creep
across the yard. What's a poem
for, anyway, if not to make the empty
spaces habitable?

A speckled starling emerges—
of the grackle nothing more is seen.

APRIL'S FOOL

I'm driving up the 101 in a U-Haul stepvan,
stepchild of my own marriage. It's 1990.
I've never seen the hills this green, never
travelled this road in spring. Wild mustard
covers the hills, its yellow antimacassars
reminding me of nature's boundless zest
for repeating itself. In the back my wife's
clothes, her records and sheet music,
half our dishes and pans. She's somewhere
up ahead in a sleek over-priced sports car.

Surprisingly the radio works. "Reach out,
touch faith." I fight it, but a wave of gothic
melancholy washes over me. Once she's settled,
maybe I'll come north & join her.
We both know I'm stuck. We both know
she's the one who leaves.

Husbands never do well in fiction.
Charles Bovary. Dagwood Bumstead.
Once we cease being lovers, we become jailers.
Poor Blondie, her abundant golden hair
piled primly, an inverted goblet, on her head,
her beautiful ankles and calves unnoticed
by her browbeaten, dithering spouse.
How she must long to unpin those thick
tresses and let them fall on that swan's neck,
those pale shoulders. How she must long
for some stronger arm to pull a brush
through the golden fleece, static leaping
in those billowing clouds like lightning.

I took my ice princess to the hills and set
her free. For me there was no going back
to the winter stream where we met.
Now I am the desert, parched and teeming
with whatever refuses to die.

KYLE McCORD & JEANNIE HOAG

RENEW EACH DAY WITH A MATCH

Daylight burns the corn
my machinations
work well in the heat & oil
in the fields
from the road passers pass
& drive. My duty to you is to rely
and be reliable
to gain passage between cows
the bright life around them
like a campfire
the way it never runs dry

JOHN MCKERNAN

THE PLATE OF SUNLIGHT

Will lift the color white
Into both your brown eyes

It will be your last supper
Your fork will stab air
Your knife will slice open the silence

The rice will not be rice but
Grains of white sand
Wrapped in an hourglass
The cooking directions illegible

The wheat will be thin & green
Waving far away in the wind
Of North Dakota ice
Your body will have the weight of a butterfly
Lugging a single grain of pollen

IN EARLY FALL THERE WERE BABY BLACKBIRDS THAT DIDN'T FORM A SOUND BUT THEIR MOUTHS WERE ALWAYS OPEN.

IN EARLY FALL THERE WERE BABY BLACKBIRDS THAT DIDN'T FORM A SOUND BUT THEIR MOUTHS WERE ALWAYS OPEN. They lived in hanging baskets hooked to our porch where their mother was often a black hole on the white boughs of the paper birch. It was at this time that you thought *miscarriage*. There is no size of what we don't know. It is, maybe, the size of the ache that only exists when you've awakened, but no one else has. It has that kind of invisibility. Allegedly, there are stars which are fires that eat themselves and sometimes plummet to earth. But the black doesn't fall like that. Think of it. If it's true, then the inside of you is a little dark museum where a painting has been removed and the lights blown out. If it's true, then the leaves are not leaves but dumb, open-mouthed blackbirds falling in the street. If it's true, then they are melon-ball scoops, falling black stars. Think of it. In the museum the white birch's wrathful roots break the marble floors. One can hear birds panicking in the rotunda.

DAVID DODD LEE

THE LORD YOU WON'T FORGIVE . . .

I measure things; the bass with the widest mouth
    gets my undivided attention,
I massage what's closest, I watch the way the pepper
    reacts in the open. I sing
to myself. I place my hands on the sheet that covers
    the mattress, time is pretty much arrested,
or I imagine the moon, neighborly with envy,
    it hooks into my body. It's sometimes
the same on top of this water, pressed to within a heartbeat
    of death, blood pouring out of my wrists
all jagged and into the clear blue sky, the lake like an agitated
    set of circumstances ringing in through the bright windows, a turtle
waiting for midnight with its claws and hopeless face, the cattails wrapped
    around the depth of things, two poachers wading around,
the pleasant heft of sinking in toward the end of things,
    the pallets of gleaming meat, the nighttime sky overhead full of
bullets and dandelions, plain coffee, the roar of never understanding;
    the releasing of the rudder.

RT SMITH

FORD FAIRLANE

(for Popcorn Sutton)

I missed my last chance to shake his hand at the Moonshiner Jamboree
in Climax, Virginia, but I was fiddle-struck by a gal with blood-colored
hair. She was singing "Sally Goodin," while I was flinging my feet wild,
and I have survived to regret that distraction, as Popcorn was the keeper
of moonshine secrets – from high shots to backings, from sweating worm
copper to proofing by shaking bead. An outlaw hero, he earned his name
with the hurt his pool cue put on a barroom's popcorn vending machine,
but he was even wiser in shadow-struck woods where the peppery jack
rises in his pulpit, where galax glows and spring water's song on rocks
is asking to be worked to the "white dog." He could take a banjo and frail
like hell broke loose, and I have quaffed a few jars of his Right Natural
to the detriment of my mind and the sweetening of my hell-bound heart.
He said he could flat-foot like a wet dishrag. He said he could smell
the snake on you if you'd been in a government building a week back.
Moonshine, brandy of the peach, corn joy – Popcorn could fire them all.
In bib overalls and his Wild Hermit beard, he'd smoke so many Pall Malls
he said a Bic would last a year, as he was lighting each from a butt's last
ember, which is partial why he made that last slow ride, curling hose
from a tailpipe back into the Ford. Pens disallow smoking, he was told,
and the judge awarded him eighteen months, despite his age, the cancer,
despite his habit of the steady cigarette. He'd rather be dead than kick
his happy habit. On the stand he said he made raw liquor of all
sorts – loving liquor, killing liquor, even the crying kind, and when
the high sheriff asked, "Which is this?" Popcorn gave him the hard eye
and answered, "This is fighting liquor, five fights to the quart, Sutton-
certified, Snitch." He said, "This is the last batch I'll ever run," again
and again, then went back past the laurel hells in his cove and rigged still
another master still to feed it fire and white sugar, corn and water.
He said, "This'll take you to the always and forever. It's hard work,
no shirker's hobby, and I don't do it for the money." On his personal
web page he'll look you right in the eye from wherever he's set down
in the greatest Yonder and gig-salute with his kinked middle finger.
Since he's gone over to ghost now, there's no way to hear him cackle
or break wind in tune or explain how he felt in himself that final
ride in the rusty green Fairlane, coasting to the eternal, and what I'll
recall forever is the scrawled note I saw in Clayton Pouncey's pool
room, signed Popcorn and saying, "If courts law me up on federal
counts, I'll fly so far nor man nor bird nor God's red daughter will
haul me back to earth. I'll go where the full moon shines moonshine

on its own, and whoever hounds me there will wake up in low hell
howling." Tipping the jug, he drained it, shouting, "Clay, fetch
my Gibson and I'll strum you the amen joy tune I call "Popskull!'"
Some say it's "myth," but trust the tale the happy angels tell,
Popcorn on the five-string, God on bass, the devil on the fiddle,
All join hands and circle left, the way the clock steals life away.
Swing that gal, stars sparking your heart and the jug in the middle.
Now he's steering that green Ford to a place where the soul gets rich.
"Bliss is why we're here," sings Popcorn. "Forget all the silly riddles
and just live, you shit-eyed whiskey-blessed son of Satan's bitch."

RT SMITH

SUNDAY SHED

How early he learned to seek solace
in the workshop where sawdust and cobwebs
never quarreled, and the blacksnake kept secret
under a brace bench and meant no harm.
If the house was a chamber of shouts

and fervor, lamps glaring, radio trembling
with sermon and witness, the ramshackle shed
beyond the fig trees offered the comfort
of resting wheels – grinding stone asleep
in its cradle, table saw with its circular smile.

Also the rake, the mute planks, drawers of dust
and hex nuts, chalk and twine. What he fled
was strife, the urge to dispute every chapter
and verse, God's words spat as arrows, grace
and hellfire testaments equal spurs for ire.

Among square and plumb, the miter box
for cutting on the bevel, the anvil black
as a Bible, he found allies and drove nails
straight into scrap pine to cover his cries.
Drowning out all babble with the hand

sander's hosanna, he learned to rely
on the spirit level with Craftsman embossed
in cursive across its steel. He would follow
that instrument's example like an apostle,
its sleeve of still water and the bubble

that seeks a balance and will not lie.

LOIS MARIE HARROD

HEADWAY BEYOND FRESH KILLS

Staten Island, NY, 2001

What was a flagging headway of salty trees
became the open sound of broken towers—
slight flashes, worn reefs–the fusty port unnosed
and sodden to the if and whether, re-schoonered.

Sinking skiff, as if you rake a book,
slug your *nosce te ipsum* boulders,
and stalk on sly. Unread stick
the craw, headway, landfill, scratching it,

and there a slow crow bobs about in the feckless
way of carrion, gagging on his chanticleer of days.
What's wrong with his *deep dazzled* larynx?
It's racking the roost of what fattens, soundboard

of raze, the groan before *I AM*, ghost in hand
worth two in the whoosh. You scold the salty cedar
and bludgeon through threadworn dune churning
grass away from the flesh wilderness of light—

can't steal atonement, not from a fetid earth,
so much waste, lamentation
that is all you sow on earth and all
you need to sow before the dark zilch down.

ANDREW COX
PLAY IN THE BOX

I left early because I wanted to get it over with

                     I wanted to get it over with so that it would be done

When it was done then I could let out some air

              The air that left my lungs said something about my condition

My condition was not helpless but required work on my part

                  My part was not central to the play in the box

The play in the box included the past, present and future accented by a ringing bell

              The ringing bell called all worshippers but I refused to come

Because I did not enter I was left to sort through what happened by myself

        By myself I found that it is never done and that leaving early is of no avail

Now leave the first person behind and approach the third person with your shoes off

              The noiseless footsteps say something about our condition

Our condition sounds like a parrot repeating our words at the wrong time

TEACHER GUIDE

Be cypress, pig-frog, red drum, be pipistrelle bat.
Spell the blue membrane between water and earth.
Conjure Sargasso Sea under your breath.
Now be spartina, now egret, be now rice-rat.
Winged, rooted, and gilled, set your charges travelling.
Feed their nerves on instinct, trusting whatever
is at hand; forget what you've been taught. Gather
your shadows; ponder their nutritious wavelengths.
Spend the year earth-bound, tangled—under
the influence of two moons, one for each eye.
Let epithet and praise float clean away,
let soil and rain make themselves into thunder
in this eat-or-be-eaten year. Now let the mess
of shapes and colors explode, now coalesce.

LARA CANDLAND

EAR SHELL

two words
in the orchards
&
porches of my ear—
what did you dram them with?
first
dissolving the cochlea
with juices of hebenon
then
dismantling
the hammers and latches
of skeleton
until my architecture
falls

i am all ghost
with no bones
traipsing the midpoint
of botanical's float

the leaves from my book
ripped out

spine open
binding
sighing

A NEW BEING

when the creature emerged

from the water

& sprouted fingers

she thought it would be good

to have something to hold—

to form a being

from the mud

& later

when the being's spirit

went somewhere else,

she thought

she would like

to stack femur

against femur

& to spread open the rib cage

to build a temple

for her dwelling

roofed with the chattering mandible

& upside down

with the lord

KATY WALDMAN

Winner of the 2010 American Poet Prize

REGARDING ASTROLOGICAL BODIES

The Greeks thought they were gods
with neuroses and sex lives.
I have little to add to this tradition,
coming as I do from the city,
from steel studded with small lights—
windows—meaning that
other windows, farther up or down
the river, are dark
like deserted hives
or lit up in reproach, being too distant
from the titans
of steel glass and cement
to do more than wave their plaintive brightness
across the water. Now men turn
to their wives and say,
"It is late" but the wives
do not hear. A dog
flips a cicada on its back
in the flickering garden.
Above there is something
that should be happening,
as when the doors close
in a theater, and silence falls.
Only here is near silence, the vagrant river
tugging its clay, chiding
"I have not done with you."

SONG

when I came home
to the house on chicken feet
my mother wore a mask with a bird's beak
and said things I could not understand,
so I dragged my duffel downstairs
to ask my father, evaporating
his hands over the stove,
and he laughed,
and the match I held startled
and caught,
a soft combustive *pop*
I took to mean I loved my father,
but not my mother,
or that it was somehow useless
to love my mother,
her forehead's lattice of lines
flaring to attention like
a wing's dark glitter
in the vasculature
of clouds.

we sat down to dinner.
like a curtain the door
fluttered open and shut,
in each crack a different
willful daughter,
a calf or an eyebrow
familiar as a flame.

I found the circling gestures
of her hands
easy to hate,
like ice crisping the boughs
on nights she patrolled
the rooms, stairs, hunting for sleep –
when the fork
and snap of timber, seized
and loosened,
kept me awake, and us alike.

Wendy Xu

The Lycanthropic Heart

And yes, the years in the wilderness are hard but you resurrect yourself
into two lives: a libertine and a specter, while I lie in a bed and talk to the Lord.
The exception to the idea of men as wild beasts is the idea of men as angels, but
we both know the lycanthropic heart. Moses once removed
his sandals slowly as a dull wind blew through the clearing, knelt before the Lord and
pressed forehead to dusty earth. Once bitten, you are in the service of love.
Once threatened by it you become it; you wake up naked on a mountain having devoured
all your flock. You don't even remember the struggle, but that's just how it goes
with nefarious acts. So like a suddenly frightened mistress I retreated, packed
a suitcase inside of a suitcase in the night. Found new commandments
while in Iowa they are burning the rows of rotten crop. Your gray wolf
padding silently through fields. A stained maw open which howls
taking what it wants. Yes, I had a den once and it was safe, but the Lord opens
his mouth and out pour other animals to take it from me.
Your punctured black sky is a face turning away.

WENDY XU

IN JANUARY STILL GONE

You say it was my going east that finally broke you. Like a switch, we are either
one thing or the other, and the middle of America is a dangerous place.

A deranged and unseasonal winter storm you blew into the coast heaving
buckets of snow onto everything. I saw it on the news, the woman in labor

cursing, having waited 9 hours for an ambulance. The baby was born and somewhere
above the city, God said give up. A man trapped inside a snowdrift wonders

if each passing day is death , but God says just wait for the thirteenth. And drink
your melting prison. Though you were never much for listening, Keith still says
        ravishment

is the halving of one person by another. No, the heart doesn't subscribe to minimalism:
it's a wendigo and feeds. God says lock it away with your other treasures, untethered

by wind, soon it's as good as gone.

OUT HERE

–after Ursula Le Guin's "Out Here"

A coyote's frozen in perpetual leap-the-razor-
wire pose

You cannot own a desert but hard water will lease you

You fishtail off-road the sky snares you with its
laugh

You conjure antelope hoofs strike alkali flats. Like
matchsticks

they kick-up the brine shrimp, & you lick
the bitter crust

You heard there is a diner but the herd has wandered

Steens means laughter while longing for a steak

When a fake creek swells you overcorrect

Three crows make a raven repairing the road. Nine
ripen a heron loose from the reeds

But a heron here
is a tame pterodactyl, a living fossil—

The desert is not an island, but an inland sea

AND FINALLY

caught the pale clouded yellows in the clover field, eight miles from home
Virginia Woolf

It is what you make of it. ache of each
you don't know who to ask

familiar music

Roof taken off. My un-mothered mother. Still

burn the garden that was, supernova that sang, distant dim plum
—doesn't last

or does it? So easy to say

"Everything that grows holds in silence a long time" when the eyes
go out of sight, what then, what when the fingers curl in the palm

one day to live. I spent it doing ordinary things, I

recall

Invisible Strings

by Jim Moore, Graywolf Press, 2011
87 pages, paperback, $15.00
ISBN: 978-1-55597-581-4

Reviewed by William Reichard

One of the hallmarks of work created by a mature artist is the way in which the maker is able to address sweeping issues and ideas with an economy of materials. A well-practiced artist is simply able to do more with less. Take a look at Carl Dryer's lovely, almost static film, *Gertrude*, or Mapplethorpe's elegant photographs of flowers, and you'll see mature style at its best. In Jim Moore's case, the material is language, and *Invisible Strings* clearly demonstrates Moore's mastery of his craft. Avoiding the gimmicky, self-consciously *avant* style that seems to bog down the work of many younger poets, Moore uses simple, provocative images to conjure whole worlds. The brevity of the poems, and clarity of language, telegraph to the reader a sense of knowing and understanding that is rare and powerful and speaks to Moore's experiences as a man and a poet.

Moore doesn't shy away from the big things here—death, love, ageing— but he takes them for what they are, addresses them head-on, and without fear. In "Friday," the narrator, an American in Italy, describes the arrival of "young Americans," and uses the moment to consider mortality: "'I miss my mother,'/I hear one say to another,/standing at a railing from which you can see/darkness coming from miles away/across the valley, the same darkness/you will be given to call your own/after your own mother is gone." The loss of his mother is a recurring theme in the book, but it's not treated in a heavy-handed or self-pitying manner. Rather, it's one more fact of life, just as love is in "Anniversary": "Reading the poet on Nothingness,/I suppose it is a higher calling than love./And yet, love/is what I have been given,/not Nothingness./Who am I to argue/with the lesser fate:/twenty-five years tomorrow." The book chronicles Moore's own ageing process, with poems addressing the fact of his turning sixty. In "Blizzard" the poet chronicles a three-day snowstorm. On the last day of the storm, he observes: "My beard grows white./I could say like waves or like snow;/but really,/white like an old man's beard."

Divided into five sections that take the narrator from Saint Paul, Minnesota, to Spoleto, Italy, around America, and "Only Everywhere"-else, this book is quiet, but powerful. Moore treats serious subjects with the respect they deserve, but also knows when to use sly humor to sweeten what could otherwise be bitter. Instead of mourning some false notion of the greater value of youth, Moore celebrates what it means to grow older, and I daresay, wiser, in "Birthday": "I ran after/the lightning bug/along the railroad tracks/the night before my sixtieth birthday,/a little drunk, unafraid,/laughing my fucking head off." Perhaps a younger poet could pull off a book like this, but I doubt it. At sixty, Jim Moore is a powerful writer. Experience, even if sometimes tragic, still comes with some reward, and *Invisible Strings* is strong evidence of this.

PRETEND THE WORLD
by Kathryn Kysar. Holy Cow! Press, 2011.
72 pages. 8.8" x 5.8". $15. Paperback.
ISBN-13: 978-0982354544

REVIEWED BY ARRA LYNN ROSS

Kathryn Kysar's second book, *Pretend the World*, takes on a variety of personas, historical eras, geographical locations, and a wide-range of forms to create a book which is broken into three "Acts," each of which set a different tonal scene. Act I relies primarily on the juxtaposition of the innocence of childhood set against the knowledge and experience of the adult heart. The fragility created by this juxtaposition can be seen in the first poem, "Last October," which ends with the lines: "in a mother's heart,/ a husk/ a silence/ a muffled cry while/ the light lies/ undisturbed/ on the horizon."

War and violence haunt this first section as a kind of circling darkness, always at the edges of the familiar world. We see this most fully in the poems "Playing with Planes," "Under a Plastic Tarp," and "Cutting Bread." "Playing with Planes" begins by describing what the speaker did not see when the Twin Towers fell, including: "the pair of business men" who "sweep/ the air holding hands" and the "silent swarms walking north." In a frightening and simple turn, Kysar sets these apocalyptic images against what she did see: "my son/ play[ing] pilot, his loud, machines/ miraculously zooming through sparkling skies." Then, she attempts to turn again by trying to enter the child mind, who "believes/ firefighters will save him. . . and no one he loves will ever die." That final turn works less successfully as the one before it by moving into a world of generalization with the lines "like children everywhere." While Kysar's specificity to gesture and setting create a strong backbone throughout her book, at times her poems are weakened by endings which fall a little flat due to their desire to tie up the package, nice and clean, presentable for inspection. While one may argue that this zipping up of the plastic bag at the end mirrors the necessary movement within the poems for order, I feel that when she lets her edges show through, her language becomes more intriguing, and engaging.

We see the language opening in new ways in Act 2, which revolves around the tension between what is wanted, what is given, and in the end, what one can do. The first poem in this section, "Bones" uses collage garnered from classifieds juxtaposed with imagery of a graveyard seen from a roadside motel, and punctuates the emotional tone by asking, "What graveyard will my children wake to?" The combination of human need set against a landscape of death set against the "delicate birch" which "give up their bones" creates a provocative emotional landscape.

Kysar makes another successful leap in the terrifying poem "The Day Ten People Died at Red Lake," which, like so many of her poems, addresses the inexplicable acts of human violence that mark our world. She uses repetition of phrases to blur together images of the natural world with the actions of the school shooter, so he is strangely compassionately encompassed (or dissolved) with his last act of suicide. The end makes the necessary leap, away from any rational understanding into pure silence, addressing the dead directly: "Ghosts singing on those stark high/ wires, we will not say your names."

The final act, Act 3, makes a redemptive move, built from both acceptance and from praise for the world one inhabits—a move that can be made only after important choices have been made, and paths taken, only after we realize that we are "trapped now in/ the small town of our lives," "having grown familiar with this landscape." Along with this redemption is, of course, the tension between the "Scrim of False Romantic Gauze" and the "Gaze Lifted," which forces us to be honest with ourselves, even if we will never know "what really happened/ inside our hearts." And so this last section is composed of love poems – the dream of the husband's lover, the lover not taken, the old neighbor who, in the middle of mediocrity, made a garden of "graceful constructions," the sister whose "hands trace the same path –" and finally, the land which is "a shell opening."

In the end, Kathryn Kysar's three acts draw the reader through an expansive world—not denying the darkness of human cruelty, but at the same time embracing the indelible and fragile "crimson" that "curls a leaf's edge." She embraces the paradox: it is only because the "earth reminds you we are all learning to leave," that you realize "these things are so good: the moon, the wine/ a silent place, the hills just behind the sky."

HONEYCOMB
by Carol Frost. Triquarterly Books, 2010.
64 pages. 6 x 9". $16.95. Paperback.
ISBN-13: 978-0-8101-2710-4.

REVIEWED BY JAMES CIHLAR

Carol Frost's eleventh poetry book, *Honeycomb*, is about witnessing a parent's struggle with Alzheimer's disease. Frost uses the recent environmental phenomenon of bee colonies dieing off as a metaphor for both the tragedy and mystery of illness. Knowing these two facts before I entered the book, and being barely familiar with the poet through journals, I expected a linear autobiographical narrative. I soon discovered that this collection is much more than its shorthand descriptors indicate.

Honeycomb is instead an ontological examination of the concepts of mind, memory, and time. In dreamlike, impressionistic language, these poems embark on the frightening quest to discover where and if objective reality exists. The riddle revolves around perception: if we lose our ability to perceive fundamental abstract conceptions, such as chronology, does that mean that those conceptions are myths? In order to subscribe to the existence of time one must experience it in the way one's peers do. In order to distinguish past from present, one must believe in memory. In order to accept the standard definition of mind one must have a mind that operates within the limits of the standard definition of mind. The philosophical dilemma of these questions is made immediate by the fact that it is the poet's mother who has Alzheimer's—

the body that gave her body life, the doppelganger of her future.

Frost's quest benefits from its deliberately ambiguous relationship with the recent history of poetics. Despite the autobiographical premise, this is not a confessional or post-confessional volume, in the mold of Sylvia Plath or Robert Lowell. In fact, it harks back to the central obsession of the modernists: perception. From Wallace Stevens' "The Idea of Order at Key West" to William Carlos Williams' "Red Wheel Barrow," modernist poems treasure the codifying systems the intellect uses to make meaning out of experience, or use language to capture the act of attention. From them, whole schools of structuralist and poststructuralist thought have dominated contemporary literary criticism. So it is all the more poignant when a contemporary poet faces the worst-case scenario that challenges basic assumptions of mind, meaning, and time, and for that matter, of poetry.

At first, the conceit of bees, hives, and beekeepers reminded me of Nick Flynn's *Blind Huber*, which uses historical research to conduct an examination of the creative process. Following that book, bees almost seemed in vogue. Again, my associations led me to expect a certain amount of heavy-handedness in the application of metaphor in *Honeycomb*, and again I was pleasantly surprised. Frost's use is hardly monotonous or predictable. She brings in the connection when it is serviceable, and sidelines it when it is not. In "Abandoned bee boxes piled on each other at meadow end . . ." she gives a clear and concise statement of the book's thesis early on: "Is it so terrible to outlive the mind," ending the poem with the beautiful (and evocatively circular) image of "time running by like a small girl running by like a madwoman" (6). In "Then it was autumn," the mother's early symptoms underscore the role of language in codifying meaning:

> —breasts, big acorns, eggs, jewelry bags?
> She waited, she told me, for the right word
> to come back to her. . . .
> (or she slept,
> intent on making time go away like a vagrant), . . .
> Honeycomb, goddess, death, fate, and the human heart,
> they lived in her until too many of her words
> flew like birds of the muses away, so few at first
> that their disappearance didn't much matter (10).

In the first half of the book, Frost shows the mother's consciousness flickering between states, still open to communication: "I said to her, there is no twenty / on the clock, don't worry" ("Two anthills and a late summer hive," 11). Set in Key West in perhaps a nod to Stevens, "You suddenly wearied. You had to sit" is a deconstructed villanelle, effectively mirroring the mother's forgetfulness through repetition. As the daughter/poet witnesses the growing symptoms of her mother's illness, the basic lessons she may have learned from her mother fall into question: "Time's soft machine goes past / spring" ("If her falling to quiet," 20) and "All history / may as well be in these brushstrokes" ("To live without memory is to have each hour," 21). What was once rigid and fixed, time, loosens, becoming a "soft machine." Whole epochs becoming compressed into a brushstroke. Time and history are now plastic and malleable. "Beauty and dust, beauty and dust" is one of the strongest poems in the collection, containing references to the river Lethe, symbol of forgetfulness in Greek mythology.

As the mother's condition begins to worsen, we see the poet's initial, and temporary, attempts at consolation: "It is restful knowing nothing / more, knowing no one any more" ("All things are taken from us," 24). A tone shift is signaled by a poem in the mother's voice, "'Generous I may have been, amnesiac,'" which includes the beautiful lines "If I went to the end of the street, / would I be at the center of my self?" (27). Although this personal narrative provides an easy way to discuss the book, *Honeycomb*'s strength and focus is the light it shines on eternal and universal riddles, as is particularly well-stated in "The humble sense of being alive":

> But if memory, as if to illustrate
> the mind was not yours to have,
> the mind was not given,
> fails us, leaving us in our underpants
> in the garden, should we not
> hate the garden,
> or the woman whose garden
> it is? (31).

Frost brings this metaphysical questioning back to earth in "She saw that the tortured dream wrestled to the floor" where Lethe is now paired with the river Styx, reminding us that death is the outcome of disease. The rest of the mother's journey, if simply in the form of approaching death, is something that the daughter can only witness, until she will later embark on it herself. In that sense, the daughter is a stand-in for the reader.

> When we're diminished to this,
> when stars are granular,
> candying a thimble of
> brain cells, how will we
> care?
> ("She doesn't see herself in the mirror," 37)

Although the trope of this book questions the endurance of time, intellect, and memory, it paradoxically uses imagination and language to glimpse an unattainable state of mind, as in "Erring   shoe   and sour bib":

> They have not brought her
> or kept her from the clamorous
>   world to the labyrinth,
> whose entrance   is age,
> for reprimand though she feels
> it, but simply
> to give her a place   to move (39)

The ending of this beautiful book reminds me of filmmaker Terrence Malick's recent *Tree of Life*, in that Frost also leaps from micro to macro. She does this in the penultimate poem, "I watched her sleep then went to the window.": "The gigantic mind that is suddenly / consumed is not less planetary." And she does it as well in the final poem, "From the somber deeps horseshoe crabs crawled up on somber shores:", in which a beach scene reminds us of our origins: the cells on the sand are enlivened by "a little spray of soul."

This short, powerful volume reaches far and wide to explore enduring philosophical and literary questions. It deserves a place alongside such recent volumes about aging, death, and loss as Louise Gluck's *Averno* and Mary Jo Bang's *Elegy*.

BECOMING WEATHER
by Chris Martin, Coffee House Press, 2011.
138 pages. $16. Paperback.
ISBN-13: 978-1566892599.

REVIEWED BY SAM WOODWORTH

In his first book of poems, *American Music*, Chris Martin opens with a quote from French philosopher Guy Debord: "Plagiarism is necessary"; at the back of the volume, Martin lists the names of those artists whose words he sampled. When I read this I sighed. Most of them were musicians I knew, musicians that are profiled extensively on NPR and Pitchfork. This unsettled me. It looked like Martin had borrowed my iPod for his playlist.

Martin's poem "I Am Not a Cinematographer" appears early in *American Music* and is a ramble of consciousness, a complex inner-life mesmerized with all the sensations of the world around. Each flowing image and thought leaps from the other, growing richer and richer until the poem crescendos with a Neutral Milk Hotel line, "How strange it is to be anything at all." This poem changed my mind about the "plagiarism." I was excited to see Martin's original thoughts swell to the same moment of awe I knew expressed in a song.

Chris Martin's newest book, *Becoming Weather*, also includes a "chorus" of voices, but this time it features fewer musicians and more poets, writers, and such brand-name thinkers as Deleuze, Derrida, Guattari, Heidegger, and Spinoza. You know, those philosophers whose names appear in texts only to remind me I should probably know more about them. The choruses in these books set the moods. *Becoming Weather* is less lyrical and maybe more academic in tone than *American Music*, but includes much of the playfulness that made Martin's first book so enjoyable.

The book is divided into three long poems—"Disequilibrium," "The Small Dance," "This False Peace," and then concludes with a "Coda." The way the poems appear on the page mimic weather. The first section is like rain with simple line breaks hugging the left margin, the second section is like evaporation with words and phrases drifting randomly on the page, and the third section is like a cloud with all of the text in a block at the top of the page. *Becoming Weather* mentions weather very little, but it's an apt metaphor for the aims of the book. It is about the attempt to feel okay with the way things always change—how nothing is ever settled and still, but exists, grows, swells, and moves on to fill space elsewhere.

The eighth part of "Disequilibrium" looks like this:

> Can I say the air
> is beautiful?
>
> Can I spend my whole life
> as a guest inside the eccentric
> balloon?
>
> Let us release
> these appearances
> and in so
>
> doing hold
> fast to what burden
> bodies make
>
> thick returning
> to us their
> unconscious care
>
> Can I spend my whole life as a gust
> outside the eccentric balloon?
>
> Can I see the air
> as beautiful?

The poem is palindromic in structure, but without true symmetry. It's emblematic of the book. The speaker starts by questioning in an abstract place, inside of a balloon, and moves by osmosis and proclamation to the outside, finding himself with a new set of questions that have shifted in shape and word. While seeking stability, the speaker discovers more instability and questions. "Guest" becomes "gust" and "say" becomes "see"; throughout the collection, Martin employs these approximate homophones and word pairings to unbalance us and move readers to different spaces. "Listening for spring // And when it returns / we will not so much // be relieved / as relived." He puts together "harness" and "harass," "steam" and "stems," "vowels" and "valves," and "scorpion" and "panopticon," all of which work perfectly as strange pairings of sound and meaning.

When this routine of similar words and abstract questioning feels a little heavy, Martin pulls back. "If refuse is the refuge of time // If philosophy is music with content // If our singing only serves / to reveal the impossible // I still want to be real / as a hamburger." He has a knack for allowing an inner-life monologue and an outer-world of simple observation to deflect and reflect each another so that neither of the worlds become too weighted. It's a refreshing balance in a book focused mostly on imbalance.

Little bits, phrases, and images recur in Becoming Weather, drizzled through the three sections. "I promise to never stop moving / I promise / to always go // sincere in the blur" comes at the end of one of the parts of "A Small Dance" as a strong conclusion—to be authentic in a shifting world. But when the same declaration appears in "This False Peace" it feels hesitant and weary, like the idea is still carried, but no longer fits the speaker. "I wanted to leave a testament to the real to things / verily happening above truth punching voices / to always go sincere to always go sincere in the blur / so if it is already happening / it is already changing." The resituation of ideas and images deepens the context and meaning. In a world of abundance and lack, like weather, people find themselves pulled in one direction or another, trying to come to terms with a feeling held in the past that is no longer congruent to where they find themselves today. We find our ideas of ourselves and how we make meaning reordering; some parts drop off, some parts come back in a different form, and somehow we contextualize an idea of "self" and "world" even though there is never a concrete and constant state of either.

In the *New York Times*, Jeff Gordinier compares the youthful poet Chris Martin with his pop culture namesake, Chris Martin from Coldplay, and describes *Becoming Weather* as an "example of a substrain of contemporary American literature that we might classify as Lazy Apartment Poetry." Gordinier singled out the least characteristic poem of the collection, a poem I noted in the margin as "interesting, but doesn't seem to fit." It indulges too much in pop culture reference and the empathy and apathy of a generation that witnesses war through television. It is a weaker moment, but to call it emblematic of the book as a whole is a potshot. If Chris Martin continued in the voice of his earlier book and accented his poetry with lyrics from the required listening playlist of any hipster, it would be a fair accusation. But he hasn't. With *Becoming Weather*, Martin is maturing and becoming a poet of breath and breadth.

MORE
by Barbara Crooker. Chattanooga, TN: C & R Press 2010.
70 pages. $14.95. Paperback
ISBN: 979-1-936196-00-5.

REVIEWED BY REBECCA FOUST

The overarching theme in Barbara Crooker's third full-length book, *More*, is insatiable hunger—not just of the body but also, echoing the opening quotation by Bruce Springsteen—of the heart. "Always, this hunger for more," the speaker says in the first poem after describing the moon as a "slice of melon, / so delicious" that she "could drown in its sweetness," so delicious that she longs to "eat the whole/thing down to the rind" (9).

The concept of "More" bodies forth in fresh and unexpected ways in these poems. In "The Winter Sea," for example, language that is pared back, muted, and rinsed of color evokes winter images such as the stand of dried weeds that, "reduced and diminished," nevertheless "remained themselves" (37). In "My Life as a Song Sparrow," life is "both more and less than I was / hoping for," one "made for song" where the body is "sometimes able to take wing" (56). In fact, more is always less here in that there is never enough of it, and the speaker, conscious of her waning years, yearns for what recedes before her vision like a slow ebb tide. But more is also a plenty in the sense that after one encounters what seems to be an end, something often yet remains. Consider the formerly despised, obese girl in "Holsteins" who "stepped out of that old life/and into another" (64). And the speaker who, after marriage, divorce, children who grew up, and children who grew up damaged, discovers on a trip to Nice "this new freedom, / slipping into a dress of silk sky, believing/I could speak another language"(45). Crooker is full of longing, but her message is ultimately one of gratitude for a world where "[a]nything can happen," and a "cow can grow wings, become an American / Redstart, flit black-and-white from tree / / to tree" (64).

In *More*, Mastery of technique is apparent in vivid imagery rendered in free verse that achieves a lyrical musicality without meter or overt rhyme. One technique borrows from jazz improvisation, repeating sounds in a pattern-with-variation. In "Geology," the title finds subtle sonic echoes in phrases like "sings one long song" and closes with a trimester rhyming couplet that uses another kind of variation on a theme:

> **Some**thing **about** eternity
> **Some**thing **about** the **sea**. (11)

Here, the stress pattern of "eternity" sonically recalls "geology" and ends that line on an unstable dactyl, a metrical teetering resolved by the last two iambs ringing through "Something about the sea." In a gesture that adds layers of richness and depth, Crooker goes beyond jazz sound arts and also uses jazz as a *figure* in her poems, as in sun "laying down its light like a jazz/saxophone lays out its brassy line" (10) and chocolate that "plays jazz at midnight, the low slow/ notes of a bass clarinet" (17).

In *More*, material taken up from previous pages is knotted into what follows in an intricate macramé in which spaces between links allow the book to breathe like a great, singing lung. The poem that precedes "Finches, Little Pats of butter on the Wing," begins with "a goldfinch bright as a grace note" (12, 13), and a cardinal appears in the poem that precedes them both (10). There are many such poem pairings and groupings in *More*, enacting in the book's form the meaning of its title. Look at how these lines from "What You Want" set up the next poem, "Ode to Chocolate" (17).

> What you want comes in five flavors,
> and all of them are chocolate:
> milk, mocha, alpine, white, semi-, bittersweet. (16)

The linking continues with the next poem's title, "Ode to Olive Oil" (18), a poem which likewise includes other images (dissipating light, an aging woman)

taken up in previous and in subsequent poems. In one facing-poem diptych—
"Demeter" and "Snapshot"—the link is thematic, both poems re-working
the Persephone myth from the mother's point of view. "White" and "Salt"
connect in the slant rhyme of their titles. The linking technique transcends
poem pairings, fretworking the book with cross and though-lines. For example,
"White's" closing line, "on that last journey home," (14) reaches back to the
exhausted runner of the book's opening poem, "walking as fast as you can
but getting nowhere" (9), as well as forward to "the cold mountain, / the long
journey home" near the end of the book (56). Likewise, the "Salt" of the poem
with that name (15) comes back later as a "salty dive" (37). Here again, Crooker
makes connections at many levels, so that the "Salt" which functions as one
poem's title, subject, image and metaphor also seasons the speaker's voice in
next poem

> What you want
> is more than refrigerator art
> more than making sack lunches

and then shows up again as "lots of sodium" in the list things the speaker wants
(16).

A powerful recurrent image is of light and all the ways it can be spent:
"poured from the dark blue sky/of a cardboard cylinder" (15), "spread on
bread" (19), "falling through the plane trees" (21), splashed from a bucket (10),
eked out at dawn by a dimmer (23), "razzl[ing]" sea water into sunset "jewels"
(37), and leaking out in the afternoon, "a letter at a time" (35). Other repeated
images are of food, the sea, summer fruit and a veritable aviary of birds whose
birdsong Crooker phonetically quotes: a cardinal scolds *vite, vite, vite* (10), a
goldfinch calls *You, you, you?* (12), and a gull taunts *can't can't can't* (37).

Another thing Crooker offers "more" of is an unflinching gaze at
the ungracefully aging physical body. Many poets, notably Marge Piercy,
have written about the way that older women become invisible to men, and
our popular culture tutors us daily that it is shameful to look anything but
perennially young. In "Surfer Girl," a speaker on "the far side of sixty" imagines
herself in the body of the surfer, "lithe and long-limbed" with "short tousled hair
full of sunshine" (27). Embedded in that daydream is the speaker's awareness
that she is really a much older woman writing a poem about surfing: "choosing
my line like I choose these words, writing my name on water, writing my name
on air" (27). Refusing to look away, Crooker describes "the cellulite, the lumps,
the bulges" (14) on bodies that creak and sag" (29) but that, insouciant, still
enjoy sex:

> Tonight there's fried chicken and sliced
> tomatoes, hot biscuits, butter,
> and peach jam. And later, you,
> next to me on the rumpled
> sheets . . .
> your sweat slick on my skin. (30)

Such material is risky in today's uber-cool, detached poetry aesthetic, but Crooker gets away with it because her writing is so strong. One technique follows the unlovely image with one that is ecstatically gorgeous, so that "creak and sag" gets the quick tonic of "a cup of moonlight/ is pouring in the window;/it glints and winks off your silver hair" (29). By interweaving allusions to art, literature or travel, Crooker opens the portal from a quiet life in a small Pennsylvania town onto a larger world. In "The Open Window," for example, the speaker enters the Matisse painting to gaze into and out of the scene framed by the artist at "slabs of salmon baking on their terra cotta/bricks, window panes, peach and melon; trellis,/slashes of mustard and olive" (47). The language in "At the Renoir Landscape Exhibit," mimetic of both Renoir's art and the lifestyle of the affluent couple with whom the speaker shares a fancy dinner, pushes at the lush edge of decadence: "The garden/in twilight: enormous globe thistles, heavy mauve cabbage roses, the scents of exquisite perfumes" (49).

The last section of *More* opens with an "anonymous six word memoir" that reads: "*All I ever wanted was more*" and returns to matters of family and local landscape: a mother who is dying, foxes who come out to make their stand on a suburban lawn. I grew up in western Pennsylvania, so Crooker's "clouds blooming like peonies on the sky's/blue meadow" and "daisies freckling the ditch" made me catch my breath in recognition (61). "Yes" reprises in eleven lines much of what the book has taught us about Crooker's voice: essential optimism and gratitude in the face of a fierce, un-slaked thirst, tough endurance, a painterly eye for minute detail, and abundant pleasure in all that the senses experience in the world:

> I want the sun to run down my face like honey.
> I want the wind to kiss me. I want all this to last (65).

So do we all, of course.

Bursting with joyous color & layered abstract forms.
Celebrating rhythm and motion.

Fine Art by Mary Zeran

www.maryzeran.com

The 2012 **APJ** Book Prize

2011 winner was **Dan Rosenberg's** *The Crushing Organ.*
2010 winner was **Quinn Latimer's** *Rumored Animals.*
2009 winner was **Mark Conway's** *Dreaming Man, Face Down.*
2008 winner was **Lisa Lewis's** *Burned House with Swimming Pool.*
2007 winner was **Matthew Guenettes's** *Sudden Anthem.*
The 2006 winner was **Theodore Worozbyt's** *The Dauber Wings.*

Who will be the author of the next book in this series? You?

The postmark deadline for entries to the 2012 *The American Poetry Journal* Book Prize is February 29, 2012. To enter, submit 50-65 paginated pages of poetry, table of contents, acknowledgments, bio, email address for results (No SASEs; manuscripts will be recycled), and a $27.00 non-refundable fee for each manuscript entered. The winner will receive $1000, publication, and 20 copies. All entries will be considered for publication. All styles are welcome. Multiple submissions are acceptable. Simultaneous submissions are acceptable, but if your manuscript is accepted for publication elsewhere you must notify The *American Poetry Journal* and/ or Dream Horse Press immediately. Fees are non-refundable. Judging will be anonymous; writers' names should not appear anywhere on the manuscript. Please include your name and biographical information in a separate cover letter. Please be sure to include your email address. The winner is chosen by the editor of The *American Poetry Journal*, J.P. Dancing Bear. Close friends, students (former or present), and relatives of the the editor are NOT eligible for the contest; their entry fees will be refunded.

The *American Poetry Journal* Book Prize entries may be sent online (save paper/postage/money! - $25) or by sending them to:

The *American Poetry Journal* book prize
P. O. Box 2080
Aptos, California 95001-2080
Make checks payable to: Dream Horse Press

dreamhorsepress.com

CONTRIBUTORS

LARA CANDLAND is the author of *Alburnum of the Green and Living Tree*. She has just released the cd Lalage: *Live on Sonarchy*, a recording of her poetry reading/singing with live electronic looping and voice manipulation with her duo Lalage. Her work has appeared in *Fence, The Colorado Review, Barrow Street, Greatcoat, Fine Madness, The Quarterly*, and many other journals. Five of her poems will appear in the next issue of *Unsaid*.

JAMES CIHLAR is an editor with Etruscan Press who teaches at Macalester College and the University of Minnesota. His books include *Undoing* (Little Pear Press) and *Metaphysical Bailout* (Pudding House Press, 2010).

LISA FAY COUTLEY is the author of In the *Carnival of Breathing*, winner of the Fall 2009 Black River Chapbook Competition (Black Lawrence Press, 2011), and *Back-Talk*, which won the ROOMS Chapbook Contest (Articles Press, 2010). She holds an MFA from Northern Michigan University, where she was poetry editor for *Passages North*, and is currently a doctoral fellow and poetry editor for *Quarterly West* at the University of Utah. Her work has appeared most recently in *Best New Poets 2010, Blackbird, Cave Wall, Hayden's Ferry Review, RHINO*, and *Poet Lore*, among others.

ANDREW COX is the author of *The Equation That Explains Everything*, (BlazeVOX [Books] 2010), the chapbook, *Fortune Cookies* (2River View, 2009) and the hypertext chapbook, *Company X* (Word Virtual). He lives in University City, MO, the Brooklyn of St. Louis, where he edits *UCity Review* (www.ucityreview.com).

LIGHTSEY DARST Originally from Tallahassee, Lightsey Darst writes, dances, writes about dance and other arts, and teaches in Minneapolis. You can find her poetic work in *Find the Girl* (Coffee House, 2010), in *Gulf Coast, Spork*, and *Triquarterly Online*, and forthcoming in *Diagram* and *Typo*; her criticism is online at *mnartists.org* and *Bookslut*, among other publications. Her awards include fellowships from the National Endowment for the Arts and the Minnesota State Arts Board, as well as the 2011 Minnesota Book Award for Poetry.

JOHN ESTES directs the Creative Writing Program at Malone University in Canton, Ohio, where he lives with his wife and sons. His poems have appeared in *Tin House, New Orleans Review, Southern Review, Iron Horse, AGNI* and many other journals. He is the author of *Kingdom Come* (C&R Press, 2011) and two chapbooks: *Breakfast with Blake at the Laocoön* (Finishing Line Press, 2007) and *Swerve* (Poetry Society of America, 2009), which won a National Chapbook Fellowship.

REBECCA FOUST's book, *All That Gorgeous Pitiless Song*, won the *Many Mountains Moving* Book Award and was shortlisted for the 2010 Paterson Poetry Prize. *God, Seed* won the 2010 Foreword Book of the Year Award and was a finalist for the Mass Book Award. *Mom's Canoe* and *Dark Card* received the 2007 and 2008 Robert Phillips Poetry Chapbook Prizes. Foust's poems are in recent issues of journals including *The Hudson Review, The Humanist, Poetry Daily, The Sewanee Review*, and *Woman's Review of Books*, and her book reviews and essays appear in *American Book Review, Prairie Schooner, Tikkun Daily*, and elsewhere.

KERRI FRENCH is a recipient of the Larry Franklin and Mei Kwong Fellowship from the Writers' Room of Boston. Her poetry has been featured on Sirius Satellite Radio and was selected for inclusion in *Best New Poets 2008*, edited by Mark Strand. She holds degrees from Boston University, UNC-Chapel Hill, and UNC-Greensboro, and her poetry has appeared in *The Southeast Review, Barrelhouse, Agenda, Brooklyn Review, Fugue, DIAGRAM, Natural Bridge*, and *Lumina*, among others.

JEREMY HALINEN is a coeditor and cofounder of *Knockout Literary Magazine* (knockoutlit.org). Some of his recent poems appear in *Crab Creek Review, Dos Passos Review, Four Branches, New Mexico Poetry Review*, and *Poet Lore*. He resides in Seattle.

LOIS MARIE HARROD's 11th book *Brief Term*, poems about teaching, was published by Black Buzzard Press (2011), and her chapbook *Cosmogony* won the 2010 Hazel Lipa Chapbook contest (Iowa State University). Her chapbook *Furniture* won the 2008 Grayson Press Poetry Prize. She won her third poetry fellowship from the New Jersey Council on the Arts in 2003. Over 400 of her poems have been published online and in print journals including *American Poetry Review, Blueline, The MacGuffin, Salt, The Literary Review, Verse Daily* and *Zone 3*. A Geraldine R. Dodge poet and former high school teacher, she teaches Creative Writing at The College of New Jersey.

ANDREA HENCHEY's MFA is from Pacific Lutheran University; her work has appeared or is forthcoming in *H_NGM_N, Absent, Muzzle, Other Rooms, Forklift Ohio, Drunken Boat, Pank, The Scrambler*, and *A River & Sound Review*. Founder of Hartford Connecticut's "Inescapable Rhythms" poetry reading series, she currently lives and teaches in Windhoek, Namibia. Learn more at www.andreahenchey.com.

JEANNIE HOAG's chapbook *The New Age of Ferociousness* came out from Agnes Fox Press earlier this year. Her work is forthcoming or published from *NOO Journal, Invisible Ear*, and *Seeing Other People*. She served as managing editor for Slope Editions and now works at the Poetry Collection at the University of Buffalo.

WILLIAM F. HOLDEN lives, works and studies Russian language at Portland State University in Oregon. At the age of twenty, this is his first official publication.

SANDRA KOHLER's third collection of poems, *Improbable Music*, is forthcoming in 2011 from Word Press. Her second collection, *The Ceremonies of Longing*, winner of the 2002 AWP Award Series in Poetry, was published by the University of Pittsburgh Press in November, 2003. An earlier volume, *The Country of Women*, was published in 1995 by Calyx Books. Her poems have appeared over the past thirty years in journals including *Prairie Schooner, the New Republic, Beloit Poetry Journal*, and *The Colorado Review*.

CRAIG KOSAK attended the Seattle Academy of Fine Arts (now Gage Academy of Art), his works are in exhibits and galleries throughout the Western United States and featured in *American Art Collector, Santa Fean, Western Art Collector, Western Art and Architecture, Southwest Art*, and *Focus Santa Fe*. Find out more about his work, including upcoming events and news at www.

craigkosak.com.

KYLE MCCORD is the author of *Galley of the Beloved in Torment*, winner of the 2008 Orphic Prize. His second book *Informal Invitations to a Traveler* is a book of co-written epistolary poems. His work has been featured in *Boston Review, Columbia Poetry Review, Gulf Coast, Volt*, and elsewhere. He co- edits *iO: A Journal of New American Poetry*.

JOHN MCKERNAN is now a retired comma herder. He lives – mostly – in West Virginia where he edits ABZ Press. His most recent book is a selected poems *Resurrection of the Dust*. He has published poems in *The Atlantic Monthly, The Paris Review, The New Yorker, Virginia Quarterly Review* and many other magazines.

WILLIAM REICHARD is the author of four collections of poetry, most recently *Sin Eater* (2010) and *This Brightness* (2007) both from Mid-List Press. He is the editor of the anthology *American Tensions: Literature of Identity and the Search for Social Justice* (New Village Press, 2011).

ARRA LYNN ROSS is the author of the book *Seedlip and Sweet Apple* (Milkweed Editions). She teaches creative writing in Michigan.

LEE ROSSI's work has appeared in *The Harvard Review, The Southern Poetry Review, Nimrod, The Sun, The Beloit Poetry Journal, Poetry East, Green Mountains Review*, and the *Spoon River Poetry Review*.

ANDREW SAGE lives in New York City, where he is Chair of the English Department at Harlem Village Academy High School (www.harlemvillage.org). Recent work has appeared in *Slice* and *Washington Square*. Contact: aasage4@gmail.com.

SCOT SIEGEL is the author of four books of poems, *Some Weather, Untitled Country, Skeleton Says*, and *Thousands Flee California Wildflowers* (forthcoming from Salmon Poetry in 2012). His poems appear in *High Desert Journal, Front Porch Journal*, and *Naugatuck River Review*, among others, and are anthologized in *Dogs Singing* (Salmon Poetry), *Aesthetica Creative Works Annual* (UK), and the *Best of Open Spaces* (forthcoming from University of Washington Press in 2011).

RT SMITH's most recent book is *Outlaw Style* (Arkansas, 2008), and new work is forthcoming from *Sewanee Review, Georgia Review, Southern Humanities Review* and others. He is Writer-in-Residence at Washington and Lee University, where he edits *Shenandoah*.

SAM WOODWORTH is a writer and musician currently living in Minneapolis. His writing has appeared in *Fogged Clarity, Thieves Jargon*, and other publications.

Craig **Kosak**
paintings
www.craigkosak.com

Giacobbe-Fritz Fine Art
702 Canyon Road, Santa Fe, New Mexico 87501 . 505-986-1156 . giacobbefritz.com

Howard/Mandville Gallery
120 Park Lane, Suite D, Kirkland, Washington 98033 . 800-544-4712 . howardmandville.com

Kneeland Gallery
271 First Avenue North, Ketchum, Idaho 83340 . 208-726-5512 . kneelandgallery.com

Mountain Trails Gallery
155 Center Street, Jackson, Wyoming 83001 . 307-734-8150 . mtntrails.net